Adventures of Jackson and Bram

Isaac Peterson

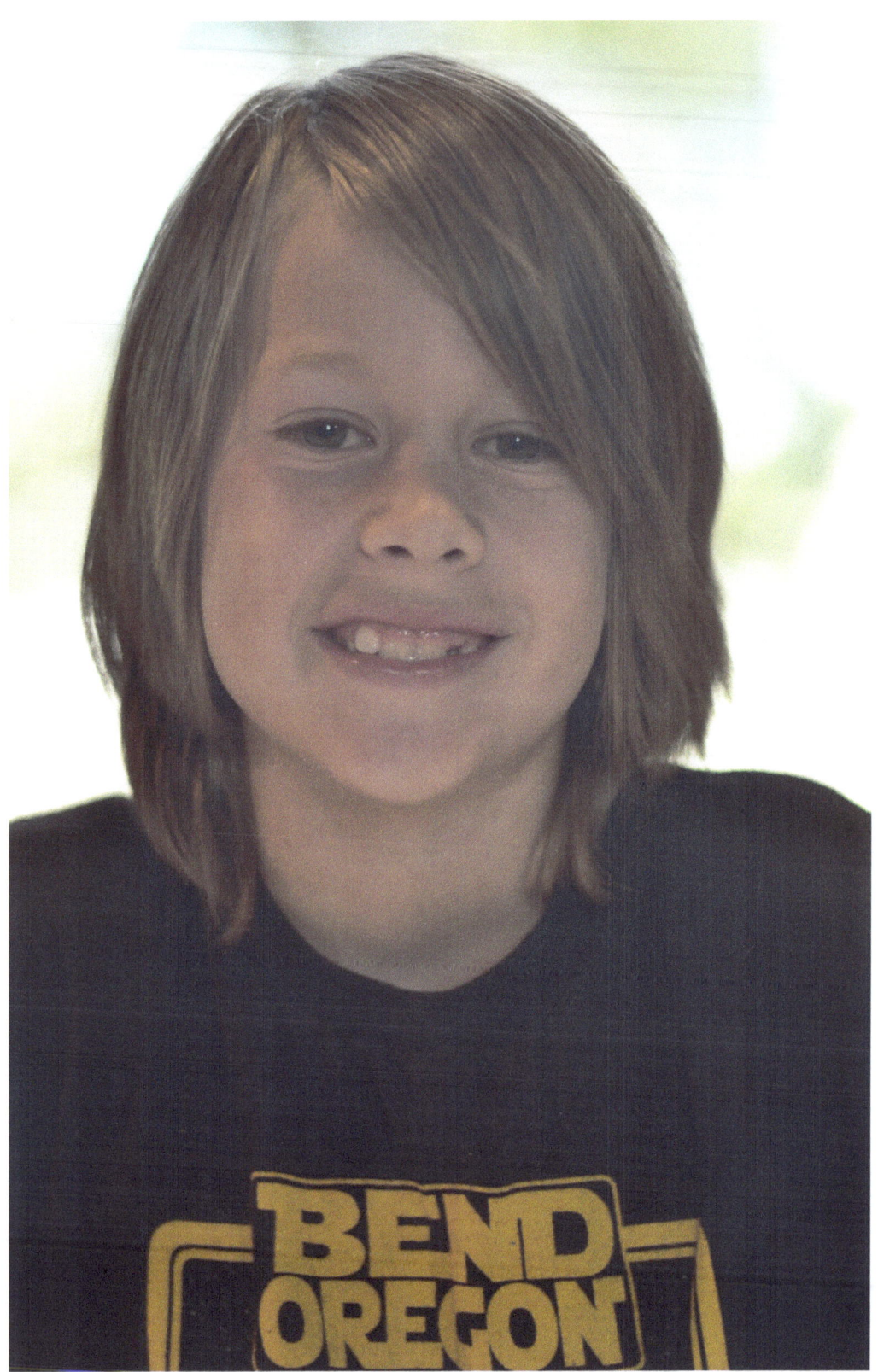

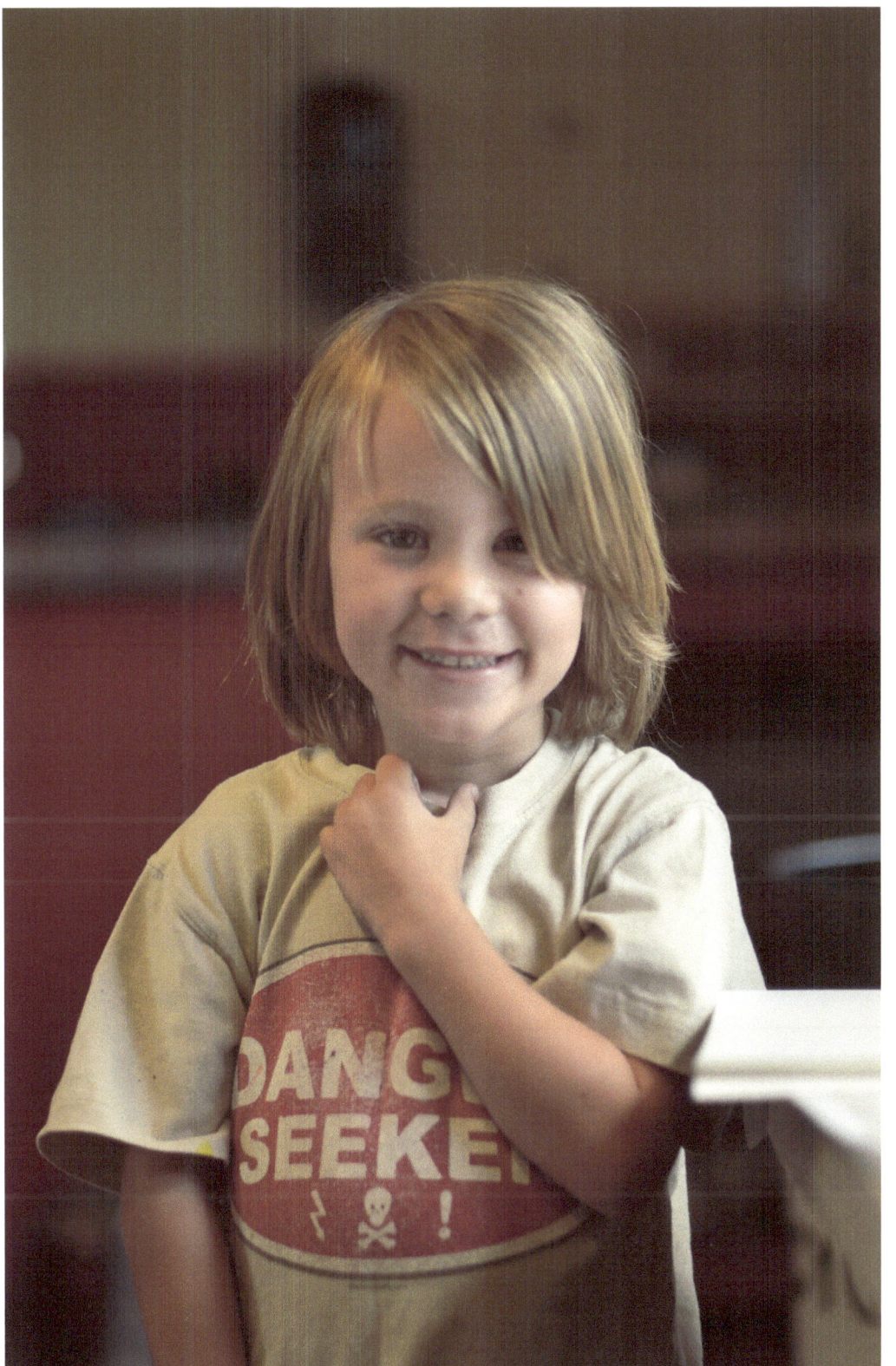

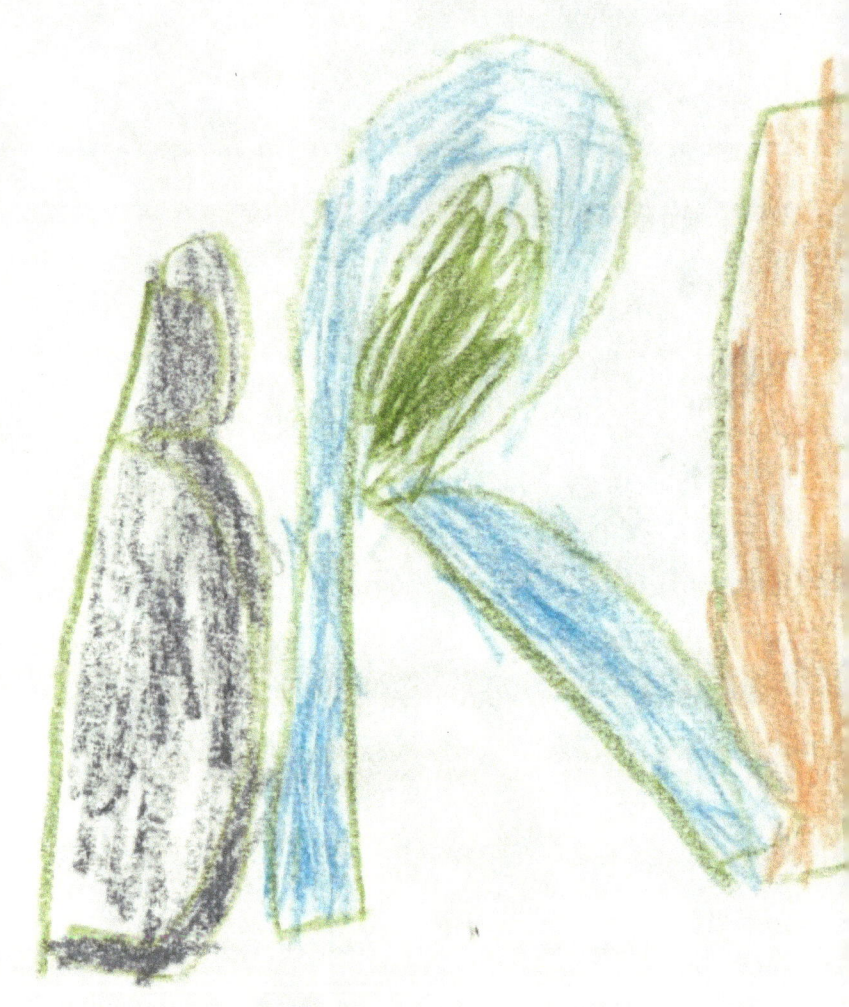

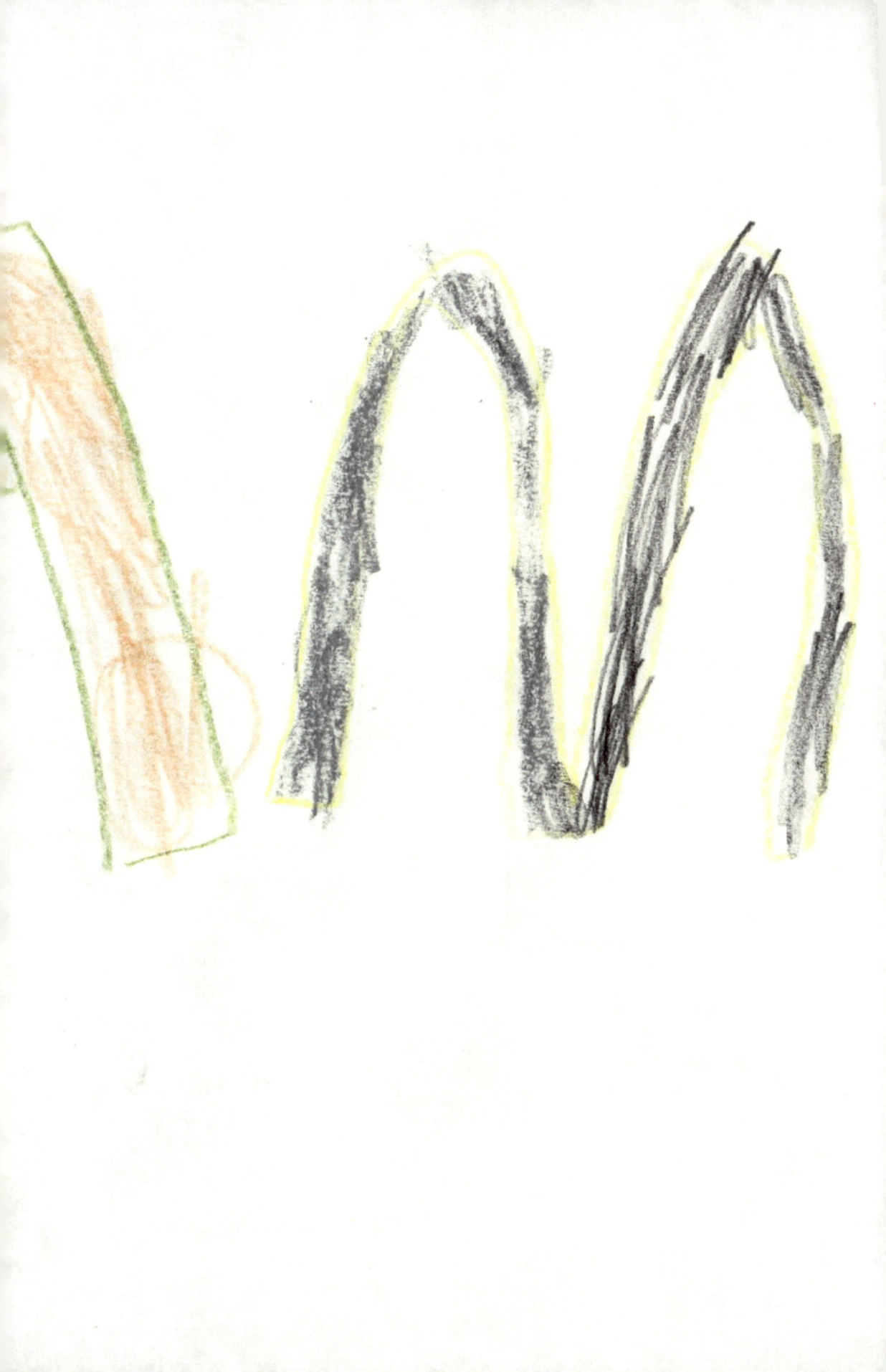

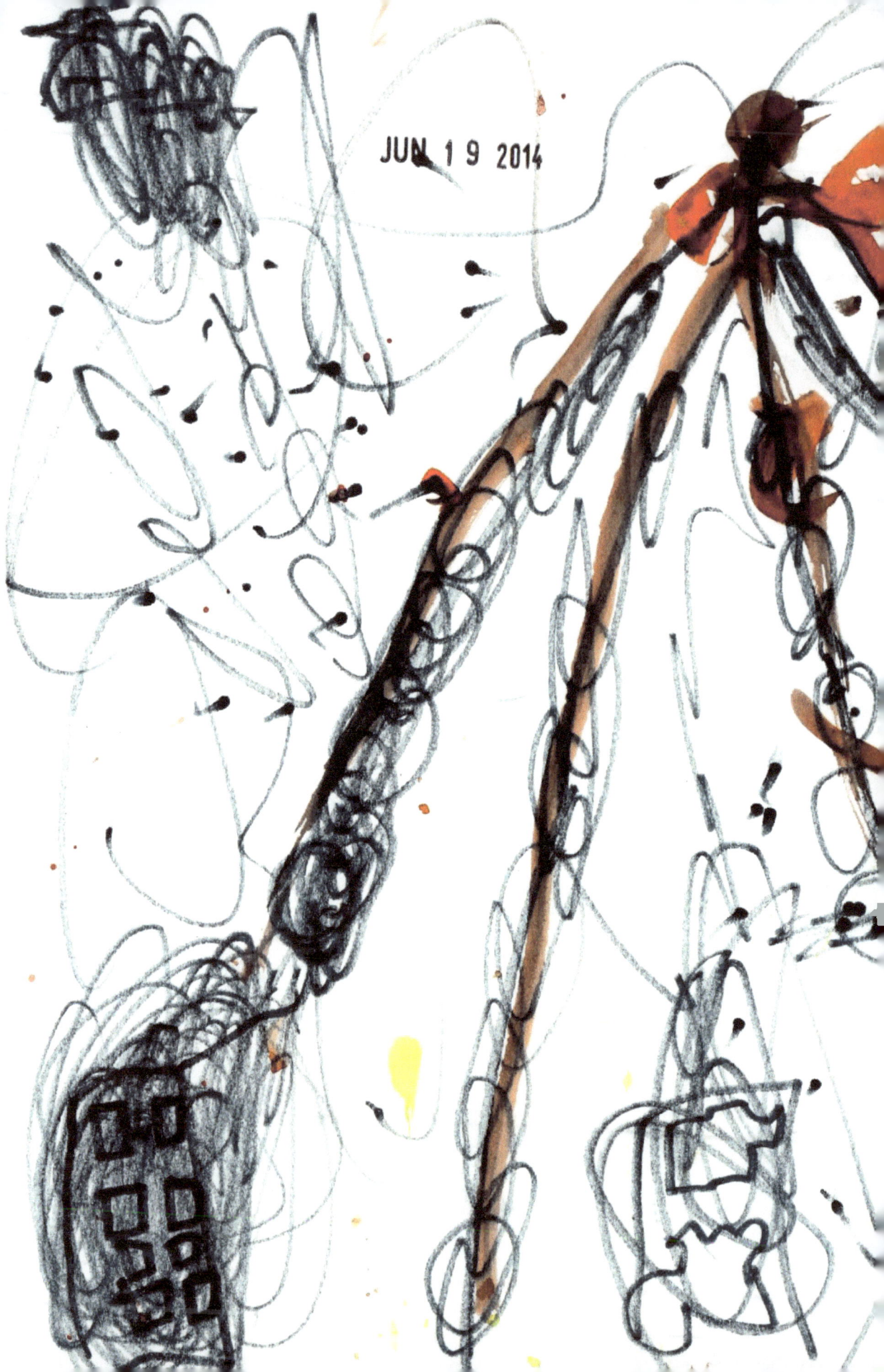

JUN 1 9 2014

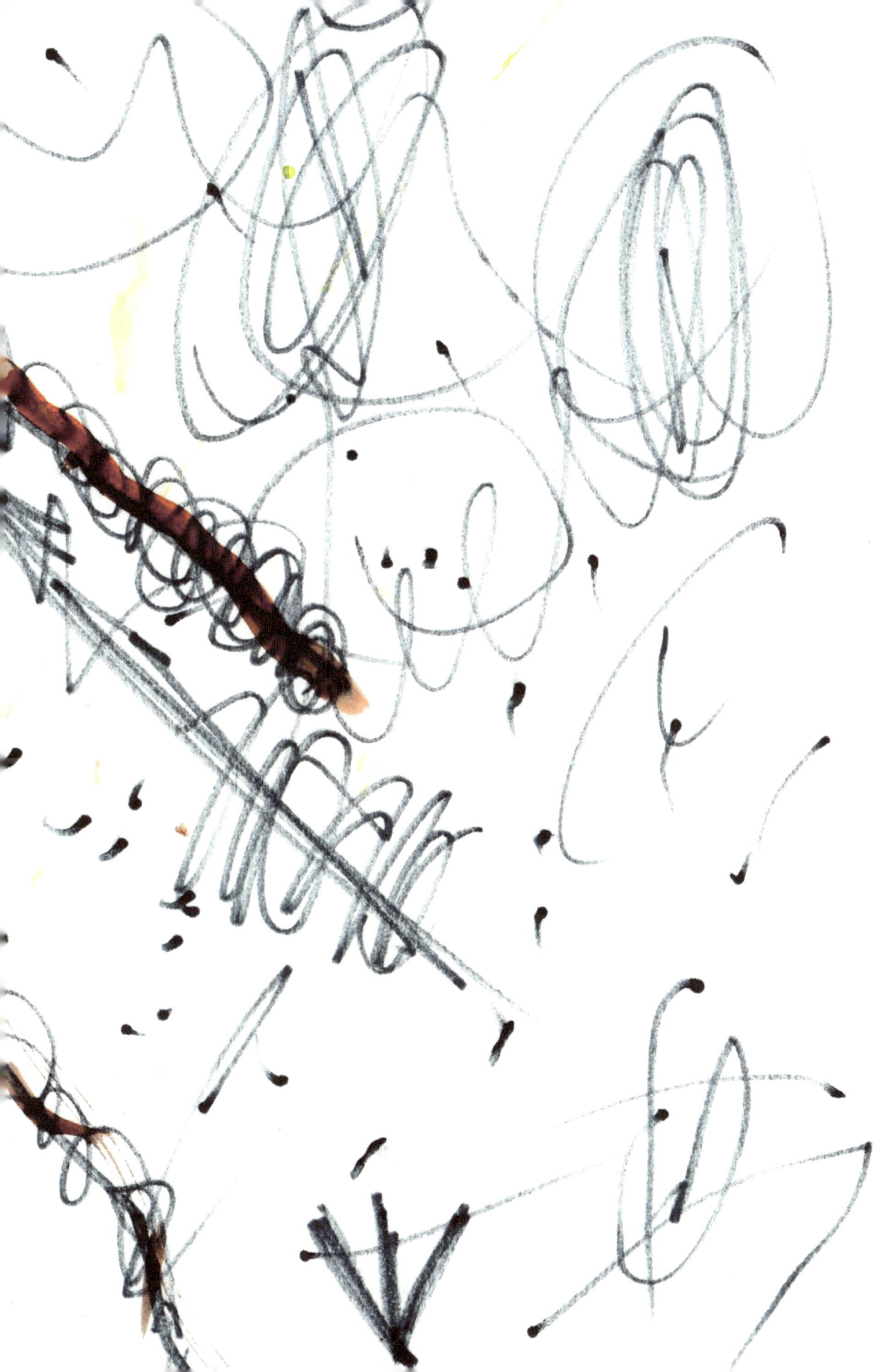

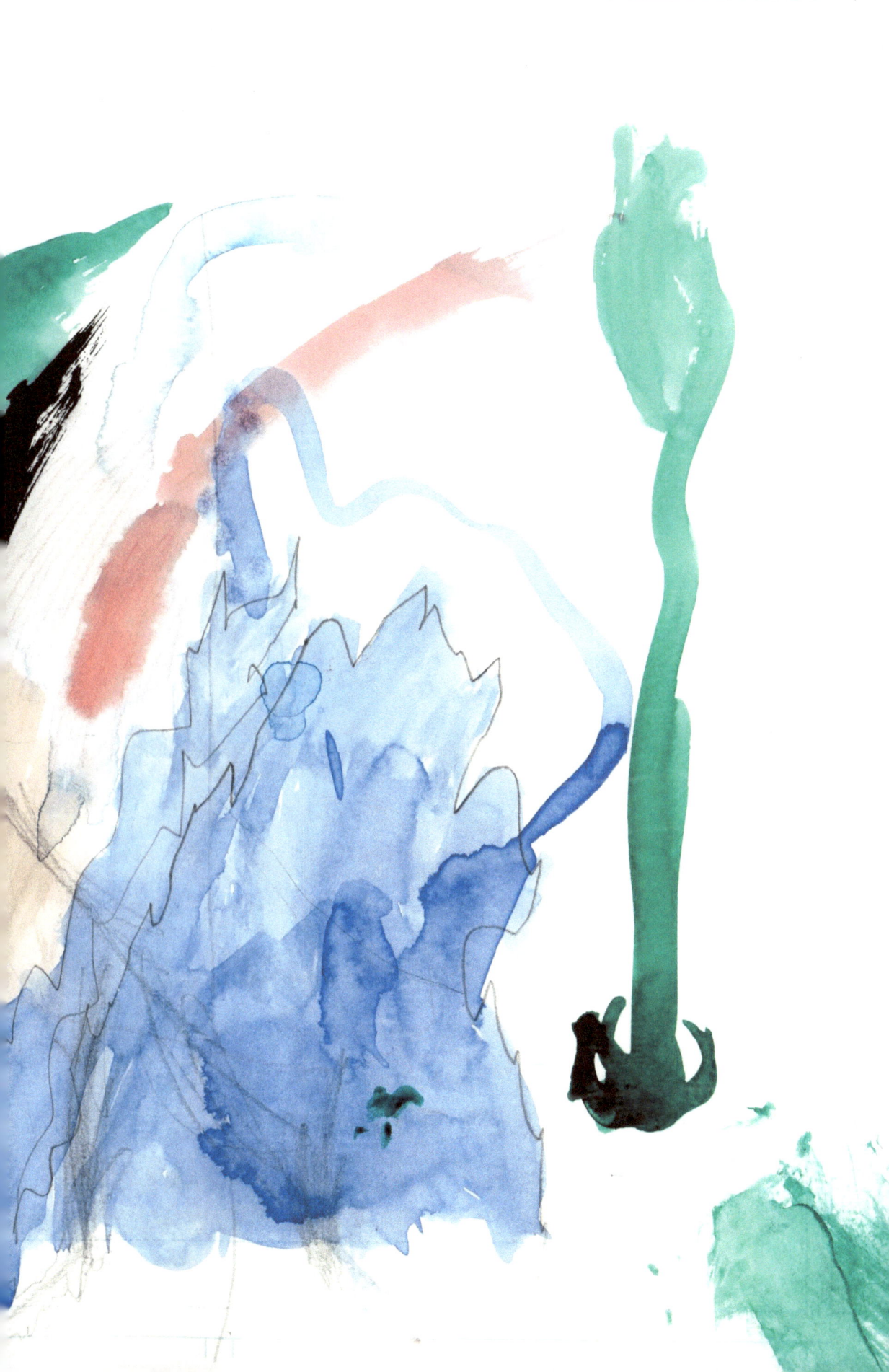

JUN 1 8 2014

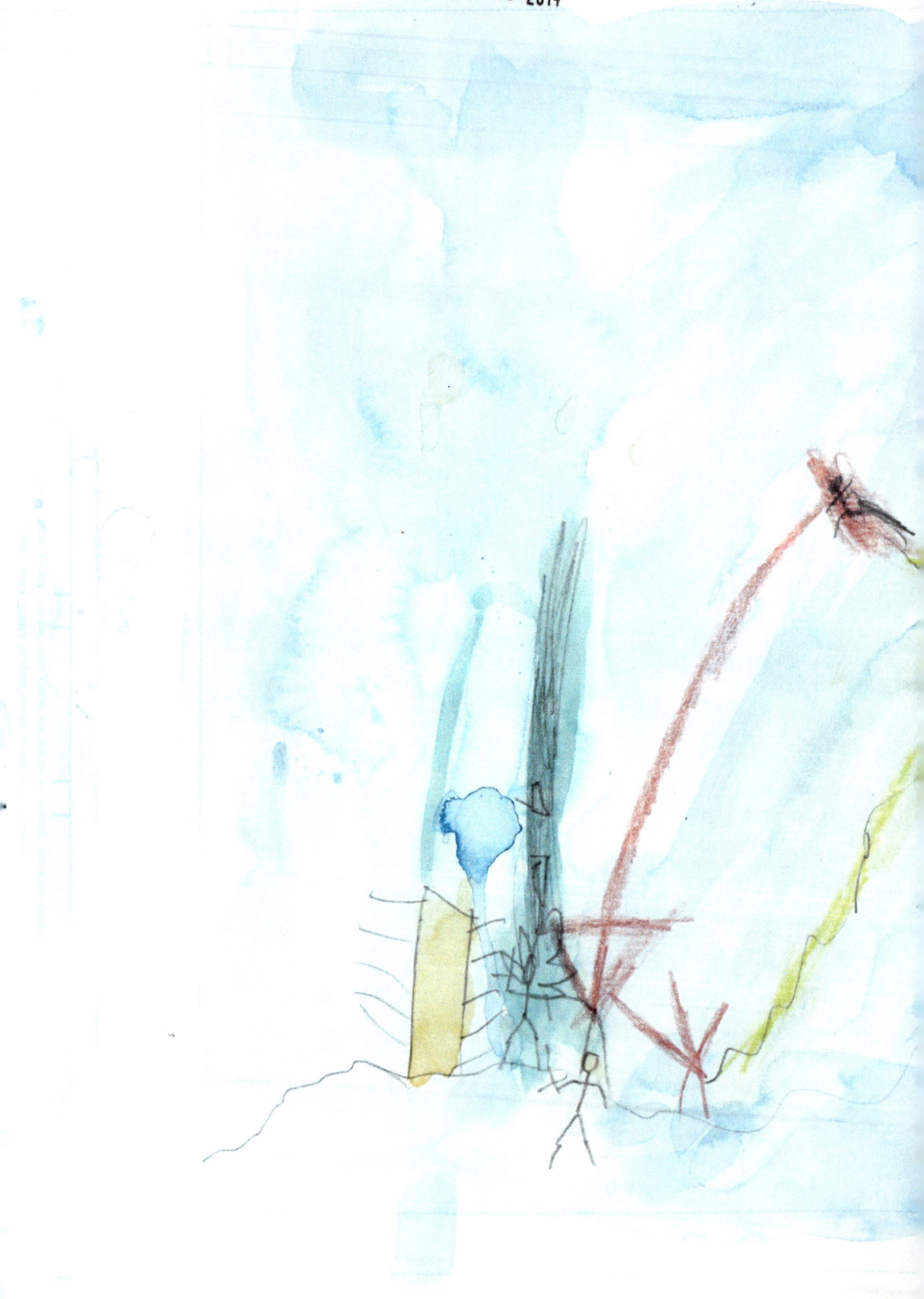

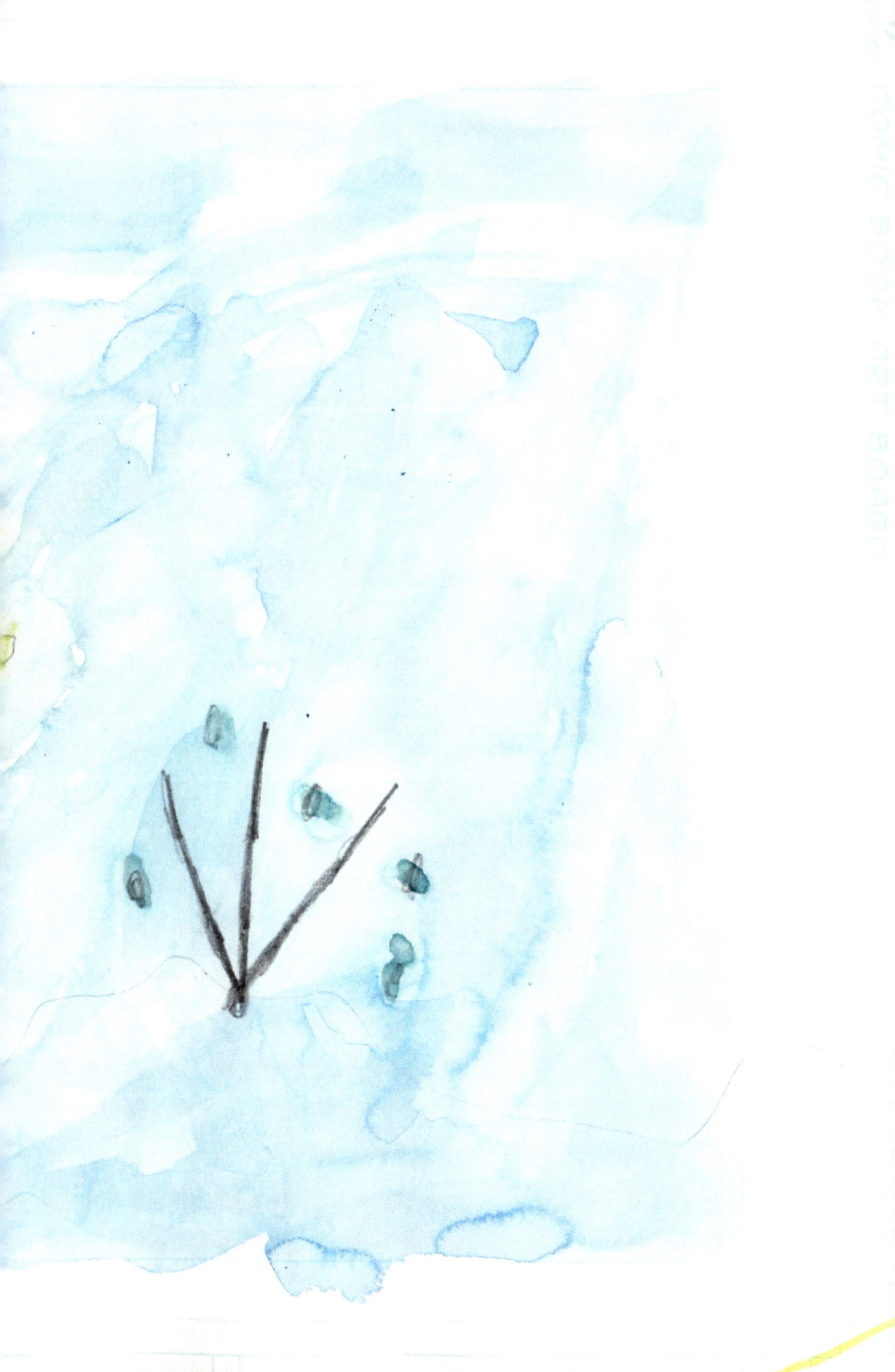

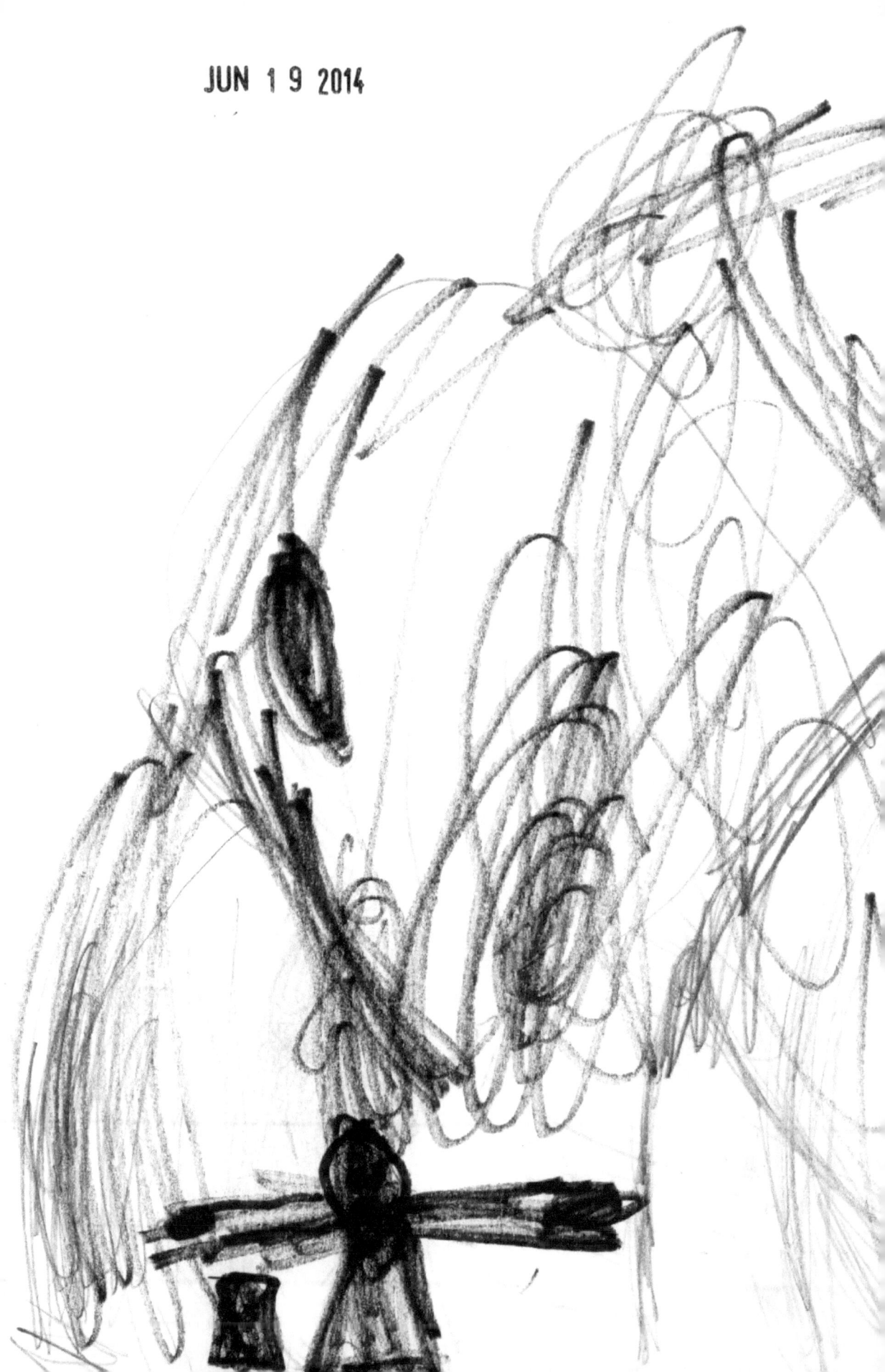

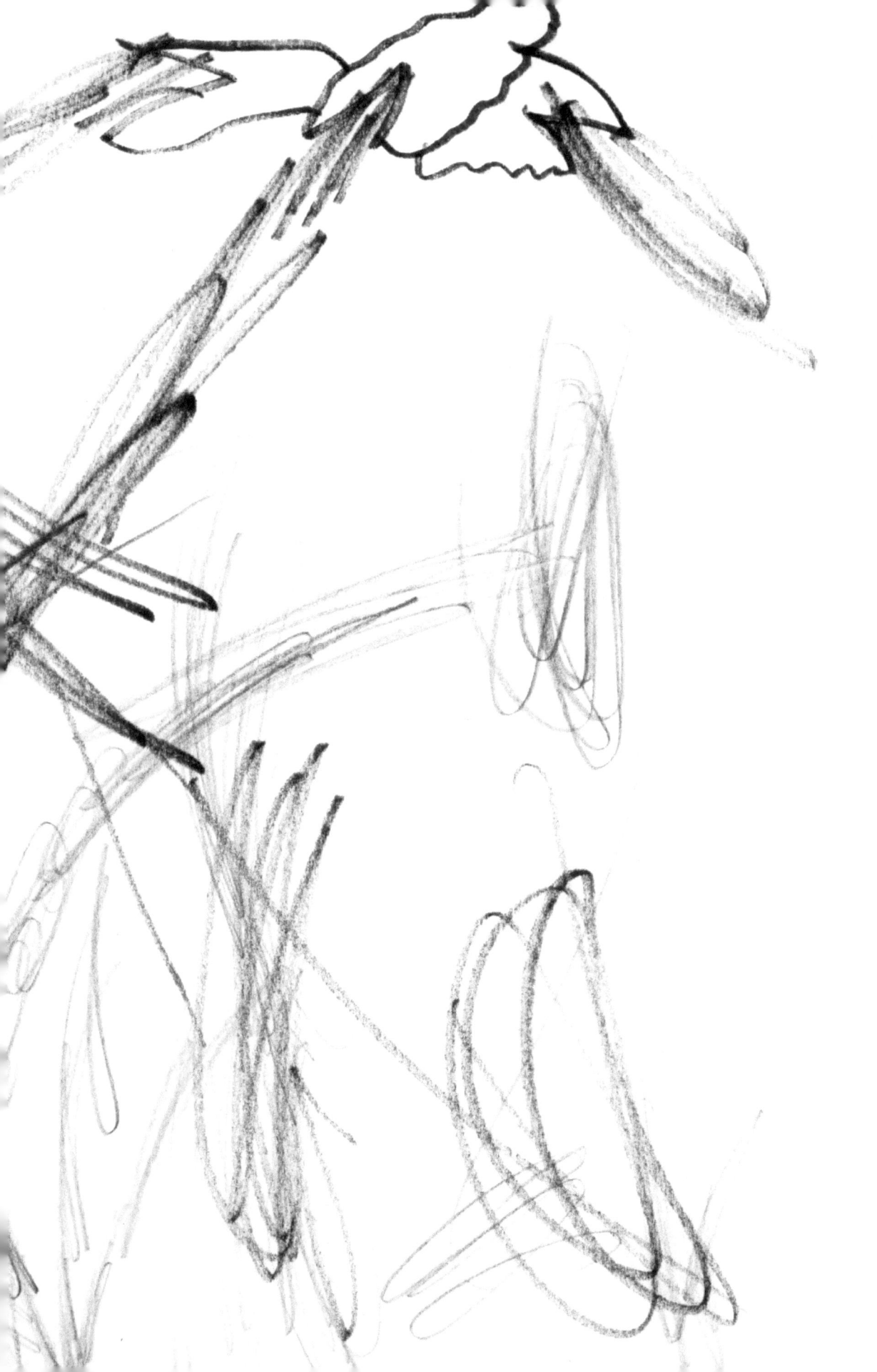

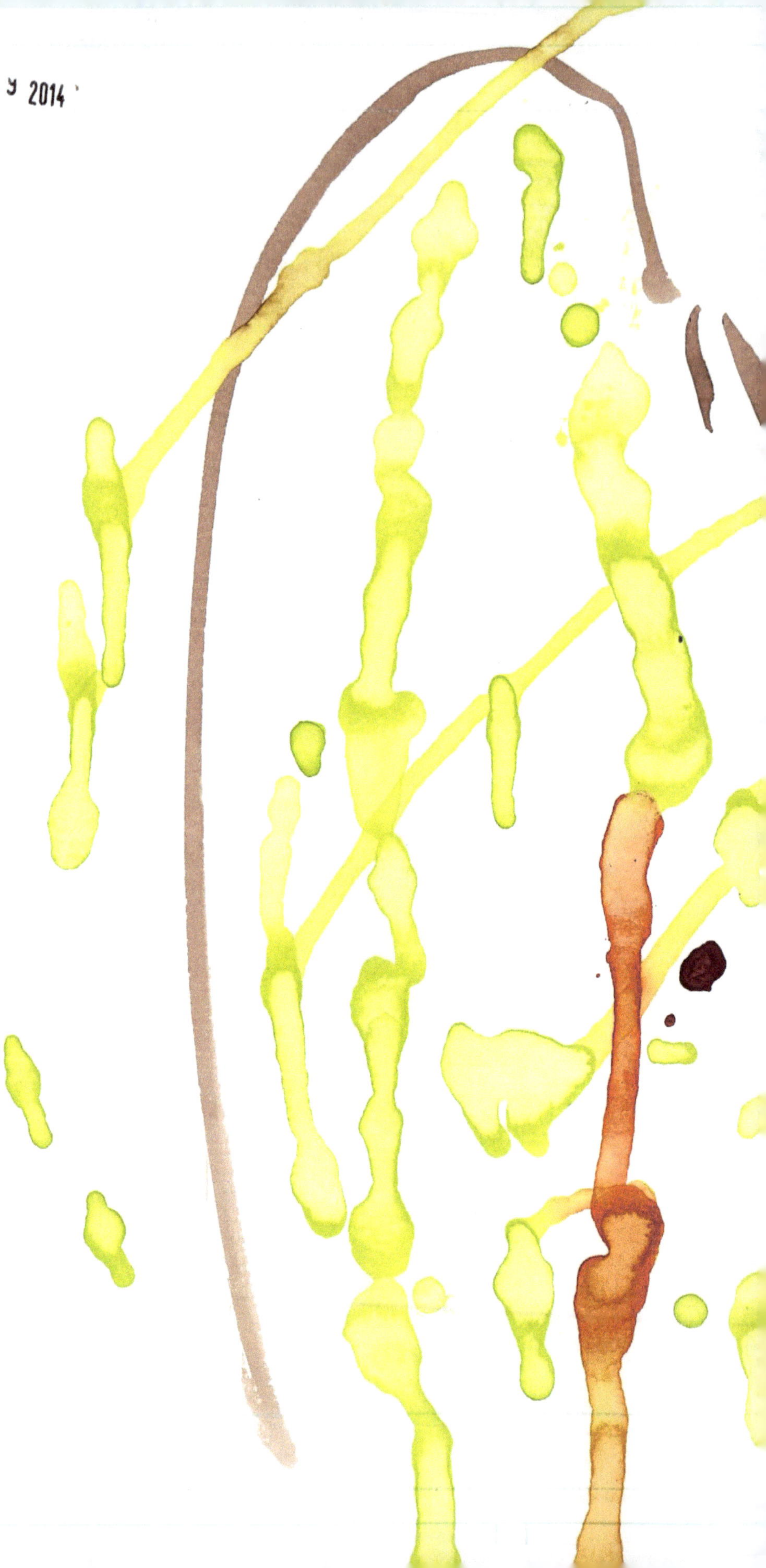

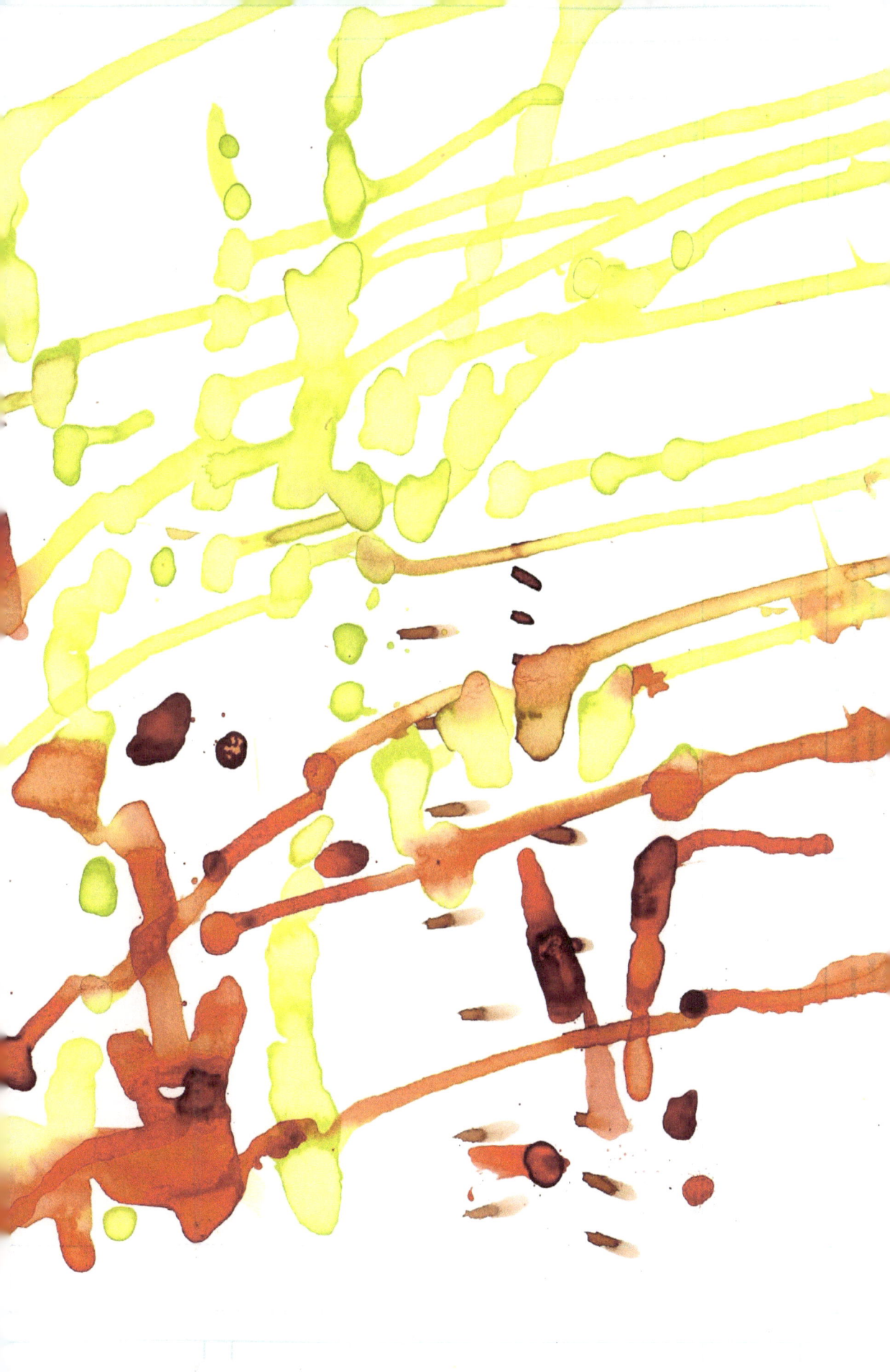

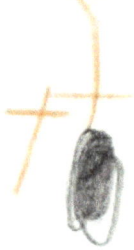

Mission -x

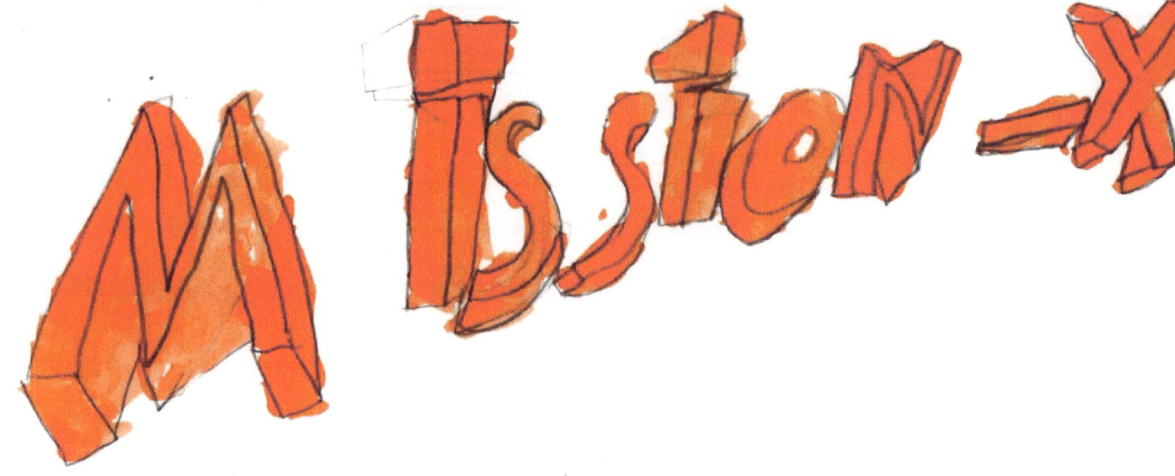

by Jackson drrakr

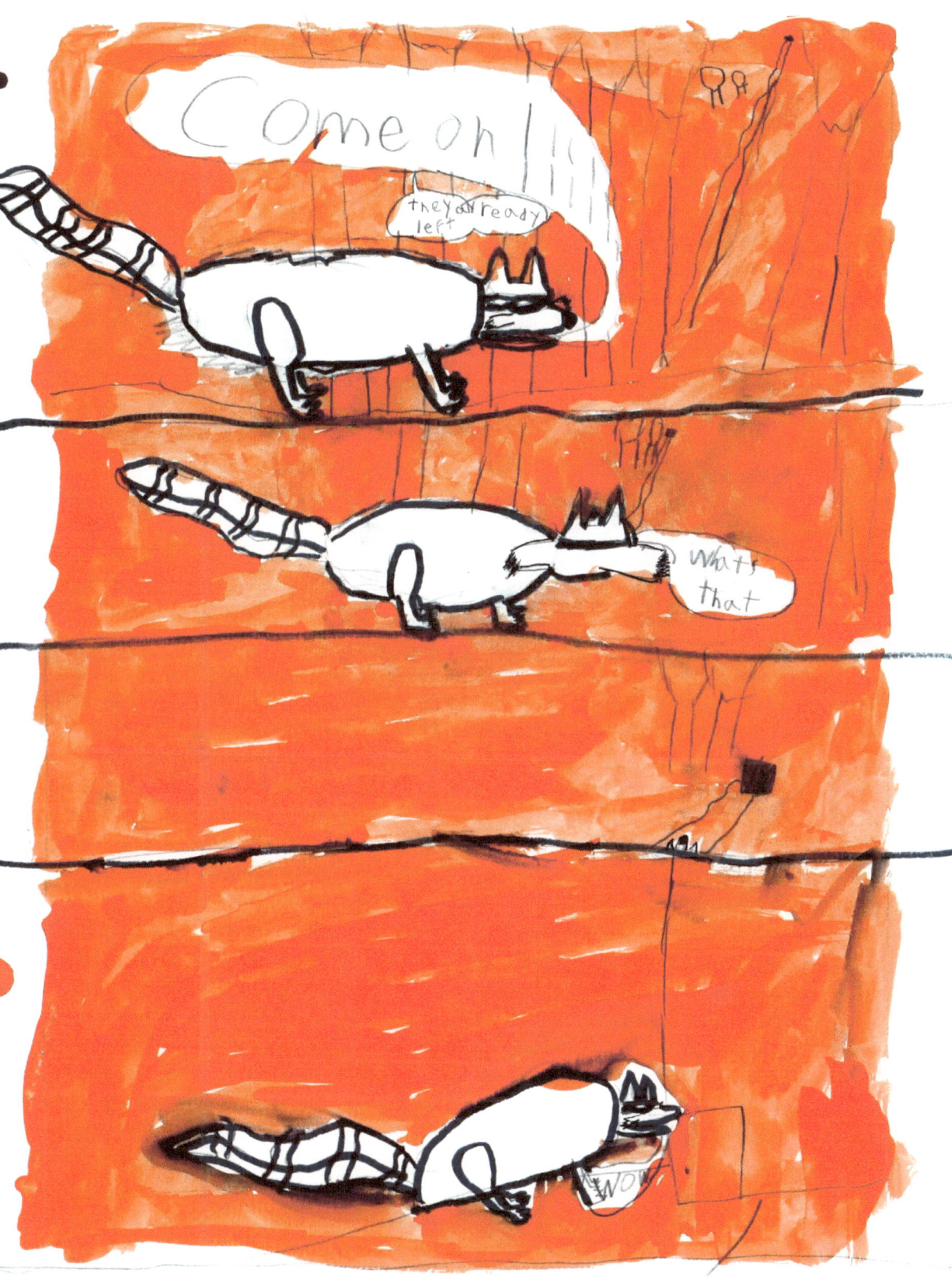

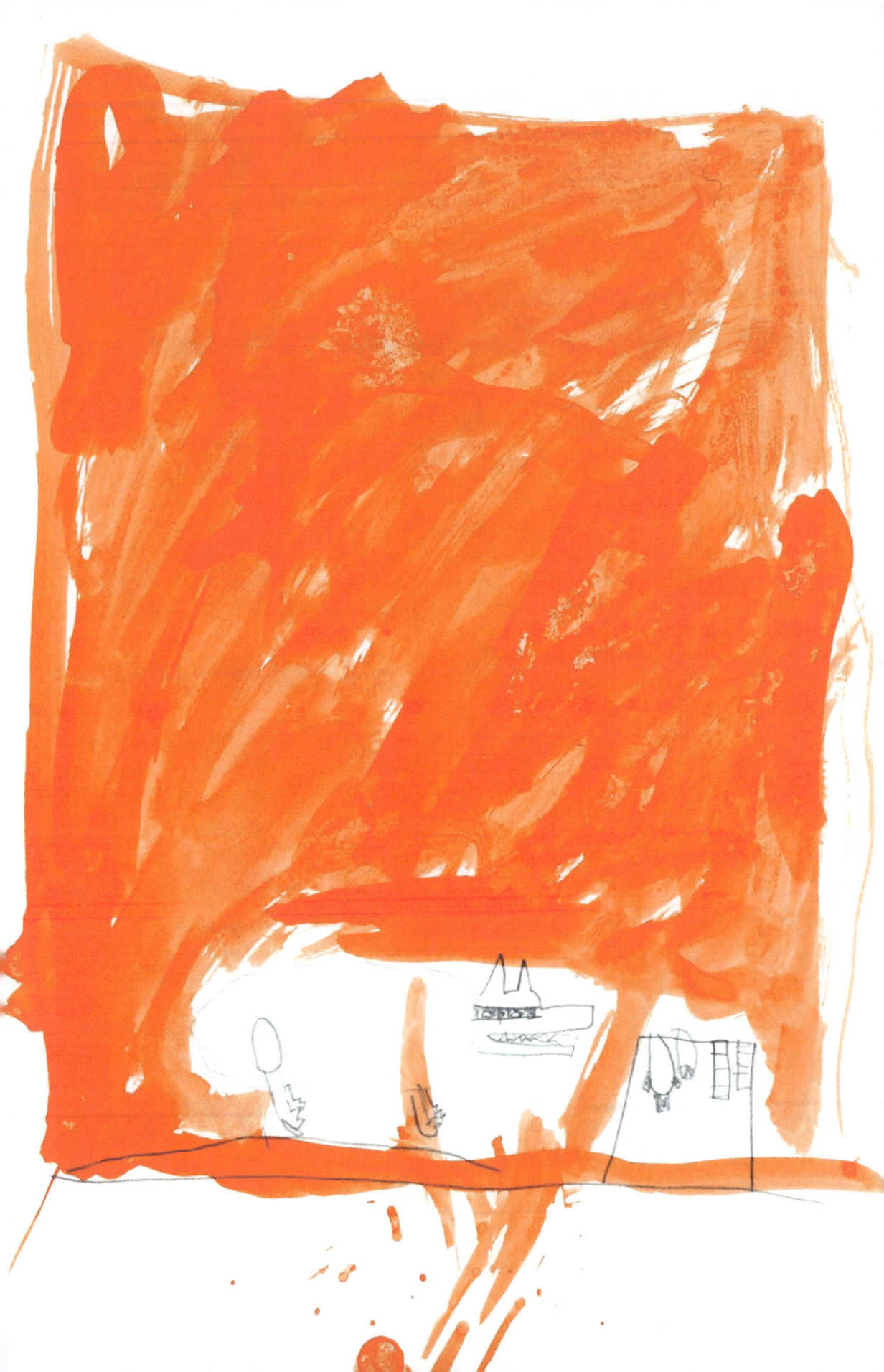

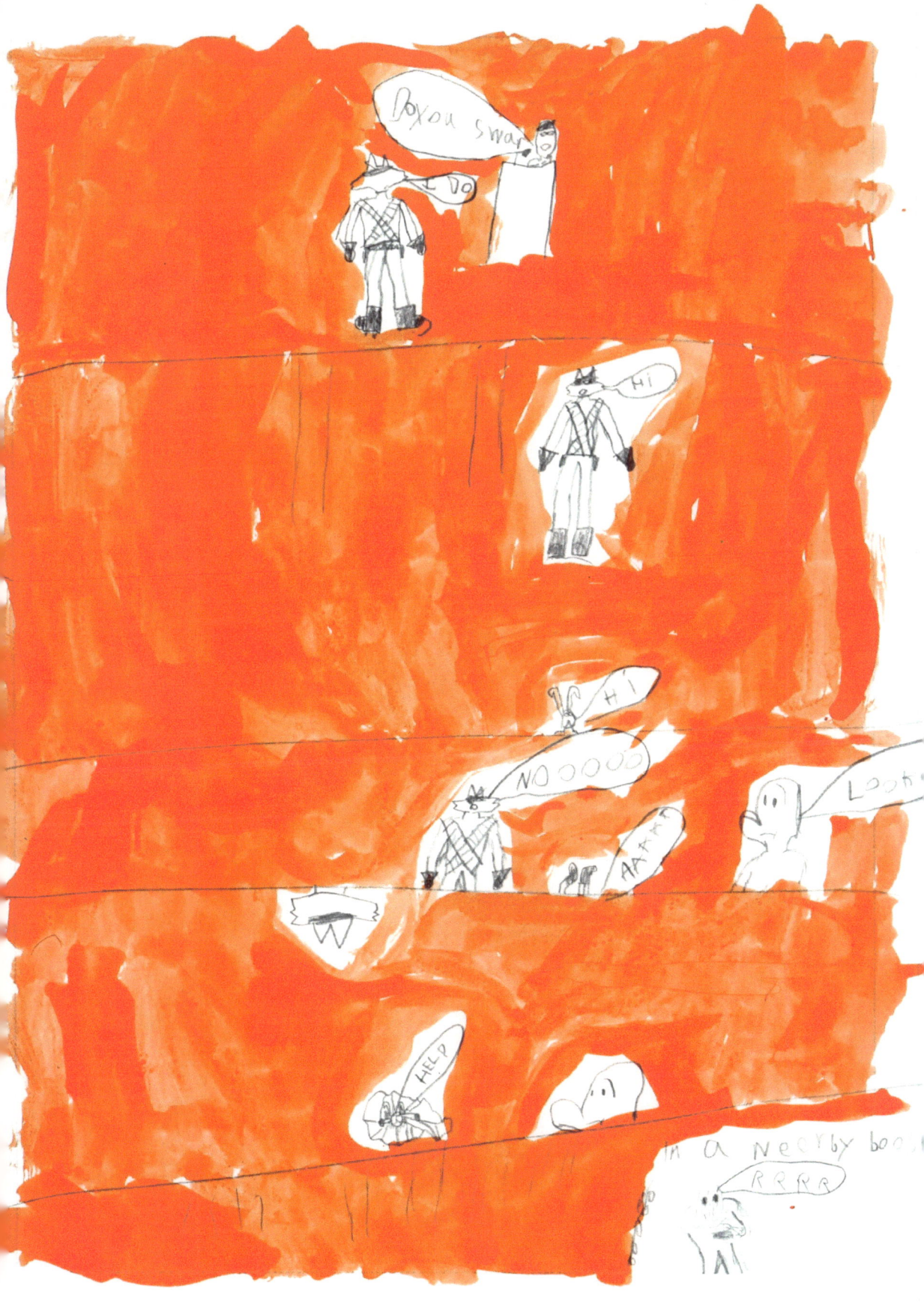

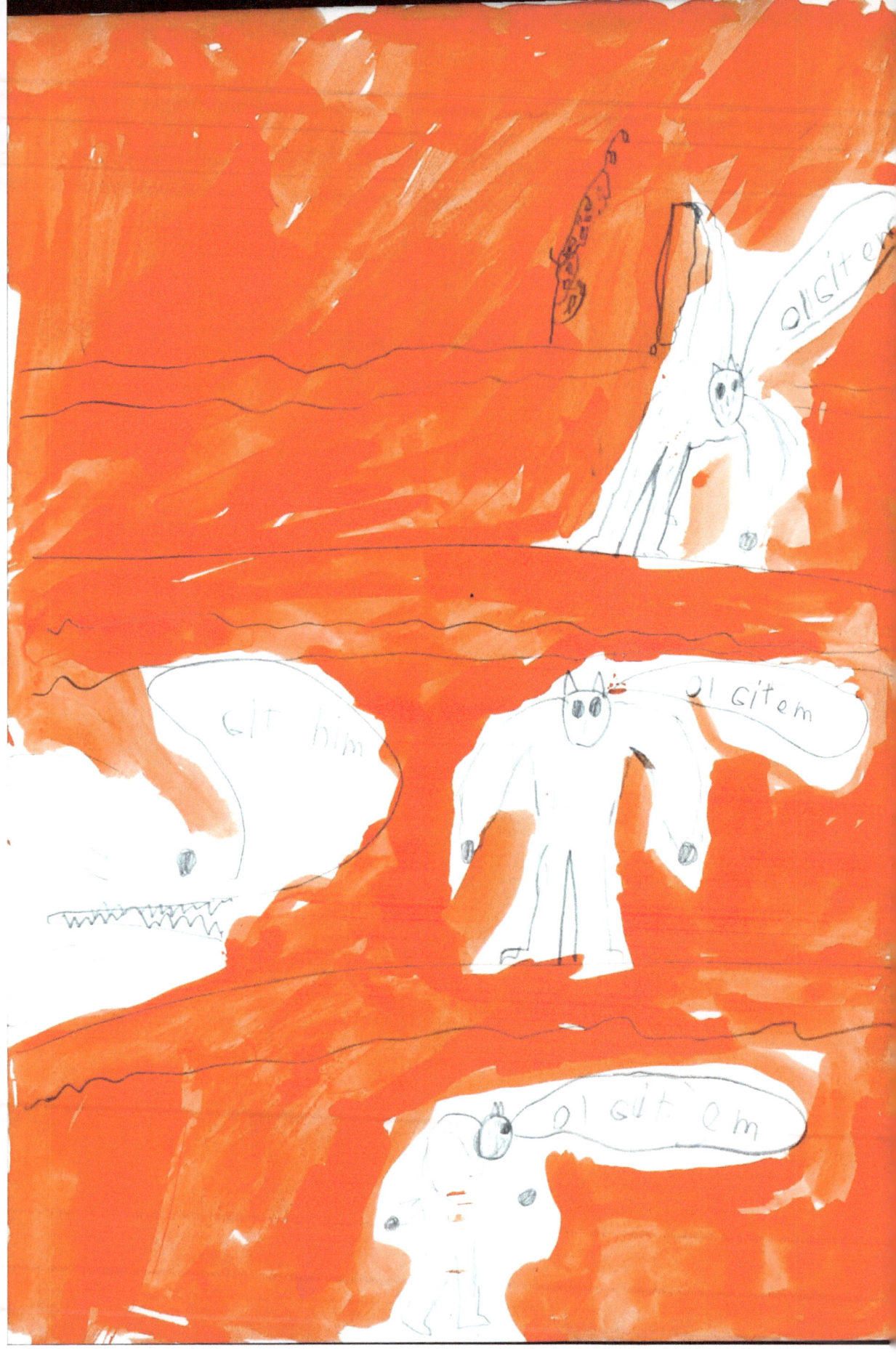

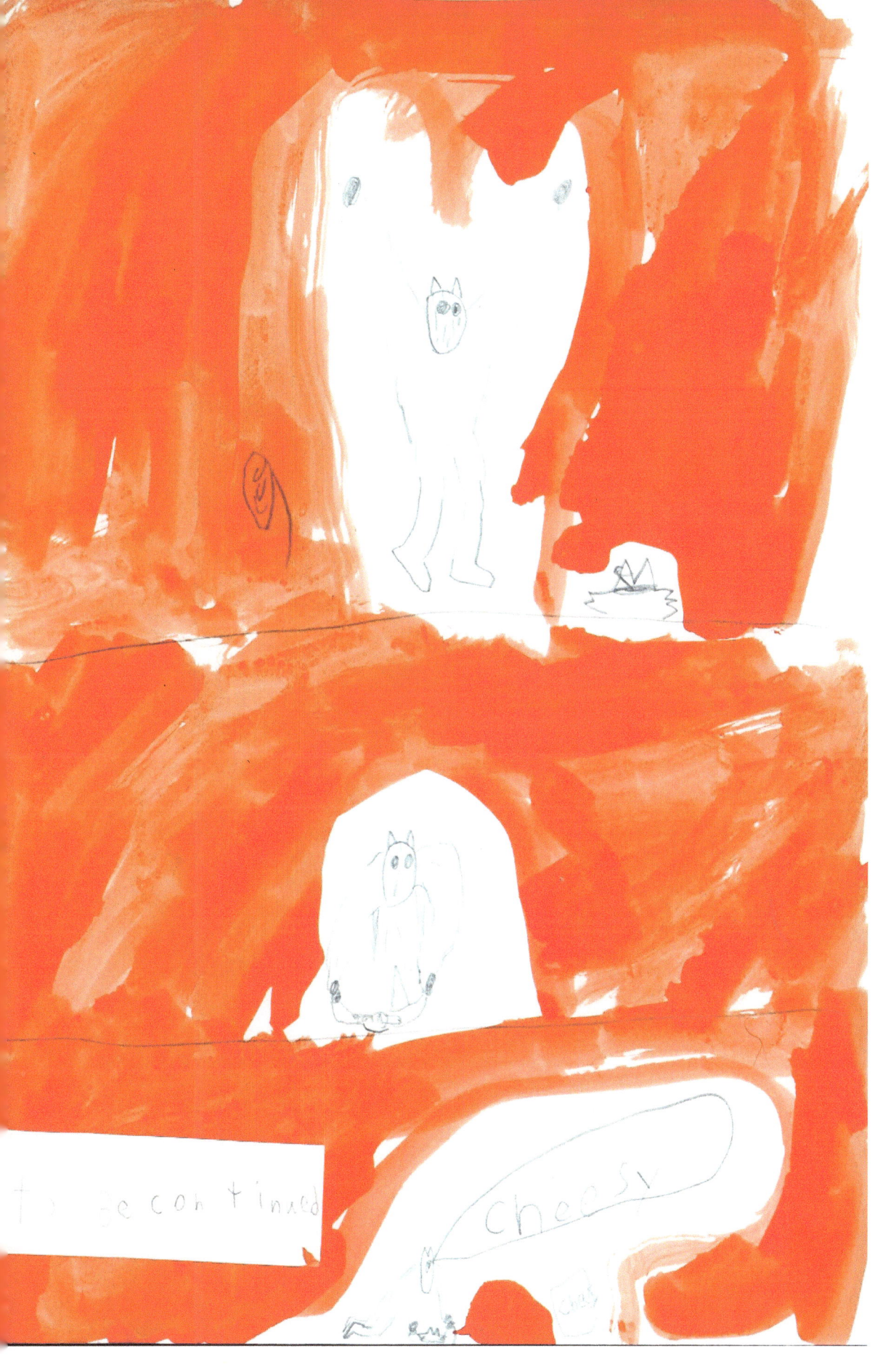

www.ingramcontent.com/pod-product-compliance
Lightning Source LLC
Chambersburg PA
CBHW050437180526
45159CB00006B/2569